How to Draw
Kentucky's
Sights and Symbols

Jenny Deinard

The Rosen Publishing Group's
PowerKids Press™
New York

Published in 2002 by The Rosen Publishing Group, Inc.
29 East 21st Street, New York, NY 10010

First Edition

Book Design: Kim Sonsky
Layout Design: Michael Donnellan
Project Editor: Jannell Khu

Illustration Credits: Tom Forget except pp. 17, 27 by Emily Muschinske.
Photo Credits: pp. 7, 28 © Kevin R. Morris/CORBIS; p. 8 (photo) courtesy of Flo Fowler Burdine, (sketch) courtesy of Bill Caddell; p. 9 (painting) courtesy of Bill Caddell; pp. 12, 14 © One Mile Up, Incorporated; p. 16 © Gary W. Carter/CORBIS; p. 18 © Lee Snider; Lee Snider/CORBIS; p. 20 © George McCarthy/CORBIS; p. 22 © Jean-Yves Ruszniewski; TempSport/CORBIS; p. 24 © Bettmann/CORBIS; p. 26 © Reuters NewMedia Inc./CORBIS.

Deinard, Jenny
How to draw Kentucky's sights and symbols / Jenny Deinard.
p. cm. — (A kid's guide to drawing America)
Includes index.
Summary: This book explains how to draw some of Kentucky's sights and symbols, including the state seal, the official flower, and Liberty Hall in Frankfort.
  ISBN 0-8239-6073-0
1. Emblems, State—Kentucky—Juvenile literature 2. Kentucky—In art—Juvenile literature 3. Drawing—Technique—Juvenile literature [1. Emblems, State—Kentucky 2. Kentucky 3. Drawing—Technique]
I. Title II. Series
  2001
  743'.8'99769—dc21

Manufactured in the United States of America

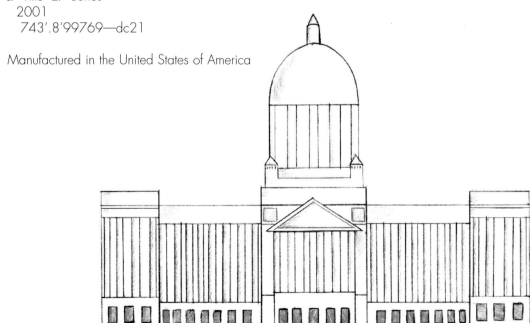

CONTENTS

Let's Draw Kentucky

The name Kentucky comes from a Wyandot Indian word meaning "plains." In 1750, a European settler named Dr. Thomas Walker first explored Kentucky's Cumberland Gap area, which opened the territory to early pioneers. From 1775 to 1810, more than 200,000 pioneers passed through the area between the Appalachian Mountains and the Cumberland Plateau. During that busy time, Kentucky became a state in 1792, and the sixteenth president of the United States, Abraham Lincoln, was born near Hodgenville in 1809.

Today Kentucky has many industries, including manufacturing, finance, insurance, real estate, retail and wholesale trade, transportation, construction, and mining. The Kentucky plains are also home to many agricultural industries, including tobacco, horses, cattle, corn, and dairy products.

Kentucky's rich and varied past has given the world bluegrass music, the Kentucky Derby, and even Kentucky Fried Chicken! You can learn how to draw Kentucky's sights and symbols by using this book. All of the drawings begin with a simple shape. From there you will add other shapes. Directions under every drawing explain how to do the step. Each new step of the drawing is shown in red to assist you. You can check out the drawing terms for help, too. These drawing terms show you the shapes and words used throughout this book. The last step of most of the drawings is to add shading. To add shading, hold your pencil to the side and draw with the flat side of the lead. You also can leave your drawings unshaded. Good luck and have fun!

You will need the following supplies to draw Kentucky's sights and symbols:

- A sketch pad
- An eraser
- A number 2 pencil
- A pencil sharpener

These are some of the shapes and drawing terms you need to know to draw Kentucky's sights and symbols:

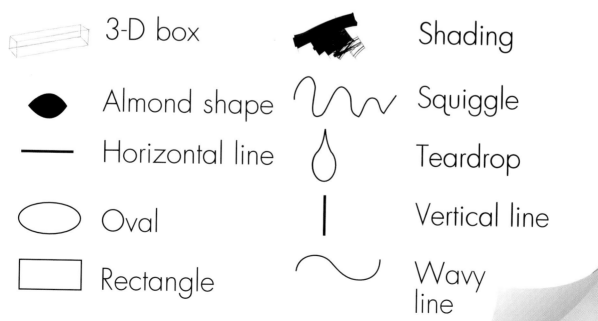

3-D box

Shading

Almond shape

Squiggle

Horizontal line

Teardrop

Oval

Vertical line

Rectangle

Wavy line

The Bluegrass State

On June 1, 1792, Kentucky became the fifteenth state to join the United States. It is the thirty-seventh largest state in the country and covers 40,411 square miles (104,664 sq km) of land. The population of Kentucky is almost four million. Frankfort is the capital city of Kentucky and 26,700 people live there. The most populated city in the state is Louisville, with a population of 271,000.

Kentucky is known as the Bluegrass State. Bluegrass gets its name from tiny, bluish purple flowers that grow on grass stems. Bluegrass also is a popular kind of music. Another nickname came from the many battles for land between the Native Americans, who lived on the land before the European settlers came, and the settlers, who built their lives on the precious soil. In 1774, a British man named James Harrod built the first permanent settlement in Kentucky. Pioneer Daniel Boone nicknamed Kentucky the Dark and Bloody Land because of these battles. Boone guided many settlers into Kentucky.

This is a view of farmland in Kentucky's bluegrass region. Bluegrass gets its name from tiny, bluish purple buds that grow on grass stems.

Kentucky Artist

Kentucky painter, printmaker, and writer William Harlan Hubbard was born in Bellevue, Kentucky, on January 4, 1900. As a young man, Harlan moved to New York City with his mother in 1915, and he attended the National Academy of Design for one year, beginning in 1918. He continued his studies in Ohio at the Cincinnati Art Academy.

William Harlan Hubbard

Hubbard married Anna Wonder Eikenhout in 1943. The couple spent more than two years living on a boat on the Ohio and Mississippi Rivers. He wrote about their adventures in a book titled *Shantyboat*. Throughout his life, Harlan Hubbard

Hubbard used pencil and charcoal on paper to sketch *Farmhouse in Winter* in the late 1940s. This sketch reflects Hubbard's love for nature. He once lived in a house without electricity! This photo is courtesy of Bill Caddell.

made more than 700 paintings, 1,200 watercolor drawings, many woodcuts, and other art pieces. Most of his work pictured rivers, river towns, and the natural world in and around rivers. By the end of his life, he had shown his work in many galleries across the country. Harlan and Anna were also well known for their simple lifestyle. The Hubbards grew their own food, fished, created art, played music, and read books every day in their small house by the Ohio River. Harlan Hubbard died in Kentucky in January 1988, two years after his wife's death.

Hubbard painted *Farmhouse in Summer* in oil on tin in the late 1940s. It measures 7¼" x 5⅛" (18.41 cm x 13 cm). This photo is courtesy of Bill Caddell.

Map of Kentucky

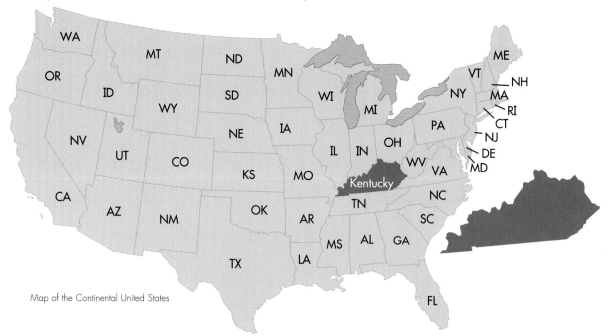

Map of the Continental United States

Kentucky is a southern state that borders seven other states. Its northern border is formed by the Ohio River, which gives the state its jagged, northern boundary. The Cumberland Plateau and the Appalachian Mountain Range form beautiful mountains in the southeastern corner of the state, including Black Mountain, which is 4,145 feet (1,263 m) above sea level. The Daniel Boone National Forest in eastern Kentucky covers 672,000 acres (271,949 ha) and spreads through 21 counties. In southwestern Kentucky, Mammoth Cave National Park is the site of the longest known cave system in the world. Mammoth Cave has more than 350 miles (563 km) of underground passageways.

1

Start by drawing the shape as shown above. Notice the straight bottom and horizontal lines, and the slanted lines.

2

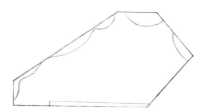

Look at the outline of the map of Kentucky on the opposite page. Then begin to draw the outline of the state with a series of curved lines. Also draw one horizontal line and one vertical line at the bottom of the shape.

3

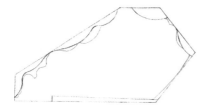

Continue to carve out the shape of the state's borders with more curved lines.

4

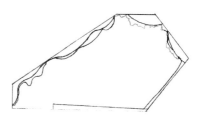

Draw detailed curved and jagged lines to create more of the state's border.

5

Continue to draw more small, curvy lines to outline the border. From time to time, look at the map outline on the opposite page.

☆	Frankfort
△	Middlecreek Battlefield
☐	Jacobs Hall
⌂	Lincoln Hall
○	Indian Knoll

6

Erase extra lines.
a. Add a star for the state capital, Frankfort.
b. Draw a triangle for Middlecreek Battlefield.
c. For Jacobs Hall, draw a square.
d. Add a square and triangle for Lincoln Hall.
e. Draw a circle for Indian Knoll.

The State Seal

Kentucky adopted its state seal in 1792, six months after it became the fifteenth state in the Union. The image on the seal shows a pioneer and a statesman shaking hands. The image represents the importance of friendship. It shows that Kentucky's citizens were unified during the American Revolution, which took place less than 20 years before Kentucky adopted its seal. The state motto, United We Stand, Divided We Fall, is thought to have come from "The Liberty Song," a favorite song of Kentucky's first governor, Isaac Shelby, and a popular song after the American Revolution. The words, "Commonwealth of Kentucky," are printed around the seal. Goldenrod, the state flower, appears at the bottom of the banner that surrounds the seal.

1

Start drawing the two men on the state seal by making two circles. Draw two slightly curved lines coming down from the two circles.

2

Begin to create the men's bodies by using long, curved lines and shapes.

3

Next draw a line for the legs of the man on the right. Also draw two lines for his feet, and a slightly curved line for his arm. For the man on the left, draw a long, bent line for his leg.

4

To define the left man's legs, finish with curved lines as shown. Finish the man on the right's arm, and add detail to his feet and coat.

5

Sketch in hair for the man on the right. Add hair for the man on the left. Then add an arm, a cuff, and a hand just below the coat.

6

Define the shapes of the men's faces with curved lines. Then draw in some of the details of their clothing.

7

Finish the drawing by shading and darkening some areas of their clothing to add more details. Erase any additional lines.

The State Flag

Kentucky adopted its state flag in 1918, although a final design wasn't chosen until 1928. The navy blue flag has the state seal in the center. The image of Kentucky's seal on the flag is surrounded by the words "Commonwealth of Kentucky." Commonwealth means that the government is based on the general agreement of all the people in the state. There are four commonwealth states in the United States. They are Kentucky, Massachusetts, Pennsylvania, and Virginia. Kentucky was the first territory on the western frontier to become a state. Today the original flag can be seen at the Kentucky History Museum in Frankfort, Kentucky.

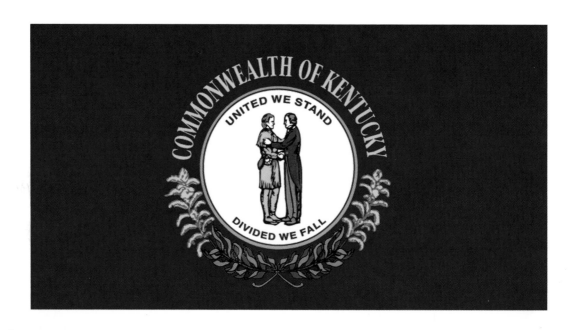

1

Start by drawing a circle.

2

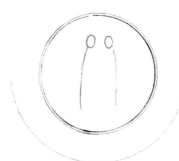

Draw a slightly larger circle around the first one. Inside the circles, draw two small circles and two slightly curved lines for the men. Draw a large half circle on the outside of the smaller circles.

3

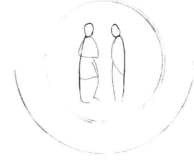

Draw lines as shown above to add clothing. Add lines for the men's legs.

4

Add arms for both men and a line down the middle for the right man's legs. Draw two curved lines above the half circle. Draw small circles for the goldenrod flower.

5

Add detail to the men as shown by the red highlighted lines. For the leaves, draw small short lines along the two long, curved lines.

6

To turn the small lines into leaves, draw them into almond shapes. Notice that some leaves are thinner than others. Add the finishing touches to the men as shown above in red highlights.

7

Write the motto, "UNITED WE STAND, DIVIDED WE FALL." Draw a rectangle around the image of the state seal. Erase any extra lines.

The Goldenrod

On March 16, 1926, Kentucky made the goldenrod its state flower. There are 125 species of goldenrods. More than 30 are native to the state of Kentucky. Most goldenrods have yellow flowers, and that is how the plant got its name. A few goldenrod species have white flowers. Most goldenrod flowers are perennial plants, which means that they live and produce flowers for more than two years. Goldenrods bloom in late summer, often in wide, open fields. These fields look like huge, yellow blankets. Goldenrods can grow up to 8 feet (2.4 m) tall and some species of goldenrods give off a sweet smell. Goldenrod blossoms are small and grow on a long stem.

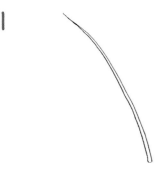

1

Start by drawing a stem. The stem should be wider at the bottom.

2

Outline the shape of the goldenrod flowers, the leaf, and the two buds. The flowers form a narrow, diamondlike shape. The buds are shaped like teardrops. The leaf shape is like a triangle.

3

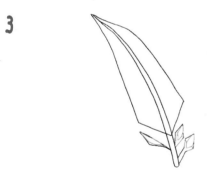

Add detail to the buds. Draw the leaf using your triangle as a guide.

4

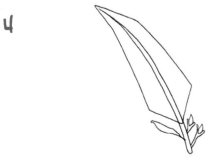

Erase extra guides in the leaf and buds.

5

Add the rabbit-ear shapes along the stem. The goldenrod flowers grow out of these places on the stem.

6

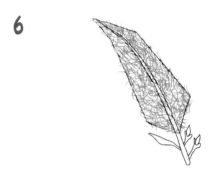

The goldenrod flowers are small. It is hard to see the shapes of each indivdual flower. Instead of drawing each flower, try to draw the texture of the group. Use repeated lines and squiggles to give the goldenrod a fluffy, tangled look.

7

Finish the drawing by adding more detail and shading, especially to the stem. Erase extra guides.

The Tulip Tree

The tulip tree (*Liriodendron tulipifera*) became Kentucky's state tree in 1994. It replaced the Kentucky coffee tree (*Gymnocladus dioicus*), which had been adopted in 1976. The tulip tree also is known as the yellow poplar and the tulip poplar. Tulip trees usually grow to about 150 feet (46 m) in height, but some can grow to be more than 200 feet (61 m) tall. Their trunks can reach 12 feet (3.7 m) in diameter.

Tulip trees produce flowers that have greenish white, tulip-shaped petals. Some furniture makers use wood from tulip trees to make furniture.

1

Draw two vertical, straight lines, side by side. Draw the right line slightly longer.

2

Then draw three curved lines to define the trunk and a branch.

3

Begin to show clumps of leaves by drawing two round shapes. Add four squiggly lines for other branches in the upper part of the trunk.

4

Draw two more round shapes to make the outlines of leaf clumps. Add two more squiggly lines for more branches.

5

Draw five more round shapes to create the outline of more leaf clumps. Make a series of curved and jagged lines all around the larger shapes to define the shapes of the leaves.

6

Finish the tree by adding shading and drawing in smaller leaves. Erase any extra lines.

The Cardinal

Kentucky adopted the cardinal (*Cardinalis cardinalis*) as its official state bird on February 17, 1926. The male cardinal has deep-red feathers and black markings around his eyes and beak. Female cardinals are a dull brown with a slightly reddish tint. Both have feathered crests on their heads and are 7 ½–8 inches (19–20 cm) long. Cardinals build their nests in bushes and shrubs. Unlike many birds, cardinals don't mind being near humans. They eat insects, grains, wild fruit, and seeds. Female cardinals lay from four to six dull-white eggs with brown speckles, usually once every season. Cardinals are known as songbirds. They sing songs with trills that last about 3 seconds.

1

Begin your drawing of a cardinal by making a large egg shape.

2

Draw a half oval shape at the top right of the egg to create his head. Draw two curved lines at the left to make his wing.

3

Next draw a curved triangle at the top of the half oval for his feather crest. Also draw two curved, diamond shapes for his feet and a long, curved line for his tail feathers.

4

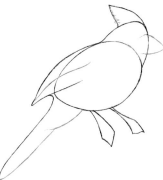

Draw a wider diamond shape to make his bill. Follow that by drawing two more curved lines to define his wing and tail feathers. Finish this stage by adding a wavy line to his crest.

5

Draw several lines throughout his body to add details to the bird. Add a small circle for an eye. Draw in the shape of his toe claws.

6

Add lines to create feathers. Finish the cardinal by adding shading and detail throughout the drawing. Make sure to erase any extra lines.

The Kentucky Speedway

The Kentucky Speedway is located in Sparta, Kentucky, 55 miles (89 km) north of Louisville. It opened in 2000. The speedway is a racetrack with three oval sides, and it is 1 ½ miles (2.4 km) long. It is 70 feet (21 m) wide. The entire Kentucky Speedway complex covers 1,000 acres (405 ha). Racing events at the speedway include the National Association of Stock Car Racing (NASCAR), Indy Racing, and the NASCAR Craftsman Truck Series. The racecars can reach speeds of 220 miles per hour (354 km/h). Racing trucks use more than 700 horsepower to go 190 miles per hour (306 km/h). The year 2000 marked the forty-fifth season of U.S. Automobile Club racing.

1

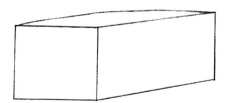

Begin by drawing a three-dimensional rectangle.

2

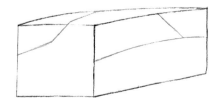

Draw a curved line to define the shape of the car's hood and roof. Also draw two curved lines on the side of the rectangle to create the side and back of the car.

3

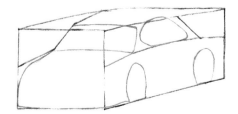

Draw long half circles on the side for wheels. Then draw a rectangle for the windshield. Draw a long oval on the side of the car for a window. Follow that by drawing a curved line in the front to define the hood.

4

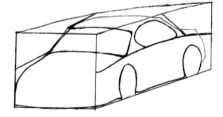

Draw a long line with a few curves in it to make the roof and back of the car.

5

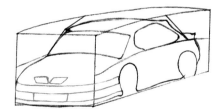

Draw two winglike shapes on the front of the car. Then draw three long, curved lines along the front of the car to make the bumper. Draw two horizontal lines on the bumper as shown.

6

Add lines on the windshield and side windows. Also draw two long, narrow ovals in the front to make headlights. Finish this stage by adding curved lines for the tires.

7

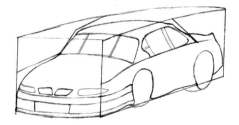

Complete the racecar by adding shading and drawing details, like a number on the side of the car. Make sure to erase any extra lines.

Abraham Lincoln

Abraham Lincoln was born at Sinking Spring Farm near Hodgenville, Kentucky, on February 12, 1809. Until the age of two and a half, he lived in a log cabin. Abraham Lincoln was America's sixteenth president, from 1861 to 1865, and he was one of the country's most-loved leaders. As president he lead the country through the Civil War. Lincoln was assassinated in 1865, while he was still in office. One of his famous quotes, "With malice toward none, with charity for all," is carved into the granite and marble memorial that stands at his birthplace. Completed in 1911, it sits on 100 acres (40 ha) of land. Hodgenville is also home to a Lincoln Museum and the Lincoln Statue, a 6-foot-high (1.8-m-high) bronze statue created by sculptor Augustus Saint-Gaudens.

1

Start your drawing of Lincoln with an oval. Add two lines at each side for the neck.

2

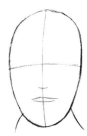

Draw a horizontal line and a vertical line to be guides for Lincoln's facial features. Add three lines in the bottom half of the face for the nose and mouth.

3

Draw two half circles for his eyebrows. Then add a straight line with a few curved lines to finish his nose.

4

Draw two curved lines for his eyes. Add two slanted lines for his cheekbones and a curved line for his top lip. Add a curved line for the hairline and two curved lines for his collar.

5

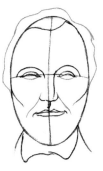

Draw two curved lines for the sides of his mouth. Add a curved line for the top of his hair. Draw a curved line for his collar.

6

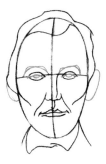

Draw small, half circles to make his eyeballs, making slightly harder curved lines to further define his eyes and eyebrows. Follow this by drawing half ovals for his ears.

7

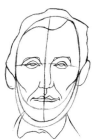

Draw two curved lines for his beard.

8

To finish add shading and detail to his face. Fill in his hair and beard. Erase any extra lines.

25

The Kentucky Derby

The Kentucky Derby, one of the most important racing events in the United States, was the creation of Colonel Meriwether Lewis Clark Jr. Clark wanted a horse race that would rival the Epsom Derby in England. He built Churchill Downs, the Kentucky Derby racetrack, in Louisville. The first race was held on May 17, 1875. A horse named Aristides won that race. Today the Kentucky Derby is held every year on the first Saturday in May. The race of 1 ¼ miles (2 km) is run by three-year-old, thoroughbred horses. More than 100,000 people watch the race at Churchill Downs, and millions more watch the event on television. A two-week celebration before the Derby includes parades and fireworks.

1

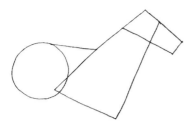

Begin by breaking down the horse into basic shapes, a circle, slanted squares, triangles, and rectangles.

2

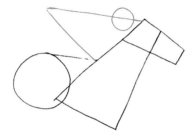

Add a circle and a triangle. These will guide you as you draw the jockey.

3

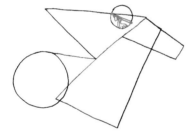

Using curved lines, draw the jockey's face showing his helmet and goggles.

4

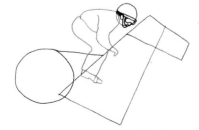

Add the jockey's upper body using curved lines as shown. Use wavy lines to draw his leg, the strap over his shoe for the stirrup, and the curve of his back. Erase the top triangle.

5

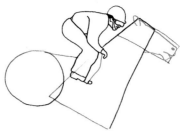

Add the rest of the stirrup. Then begin working on the horse's face. Draw the ear using part of an oval, the nostril using a filled-in circle, and the mouth using curved, wavy lines.

6

Draw the horse's mane using lots of lines. Then draw his chest with a slanted line. Draw straps using slanted lines and a circle.

7

Draw the rear end of the horse using curved lines. Then add the legs as shown.

8

Draw the horse's tail and the saddle. Then add shading and detail. Erase any extra lines.

Kentucky's Capitol

Kentucky's state capitol building in Frankfort is the state's fourth capitol building since 1792. The first two buildings were ruined by fires. The third capitol building still stands and has been named a National Historic Landmark. The current capitol, designed by architect Frank Mills Andrews, was completed in 1910. Its Beaux Arts style of architecture combines Greek and French designs. A statue of Abraham Lincoln stands in its rotunda. Other statues of famous Kentuckians include Senator Henry Clay (1777–1852), Jefferson Davis, president of the Confederate States during the Civil War (1861–1865), and Alben William Barkley, vice president under U.S. President Harry S. Truman (1949–1953).

1

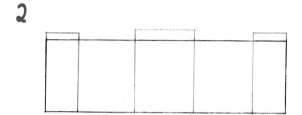

Start by drawing a large rectangle.

2

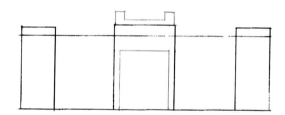

Then draw three smaller rectangles with one in the middle and one on either end.

3

Draw a box in the center rectangle. Next draw a shape at the top of the center rectangle as shown.

4

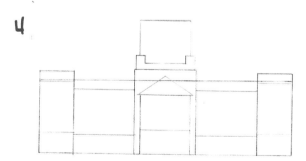

To begin the dome, draw a box on the top of this structure. Add a triangle above the center box. Finish by drawing nine lines.

5

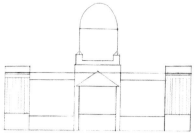

Draw a large half circle for the dome. Add two small triangles on the roof, and draw lines for columns in both side rectangles.

6

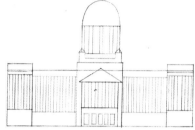

Draw lines to create columns in the dome and center of the building. Add five rectangles at the entrance of the building.

7

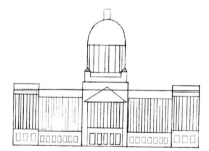

Add windows by drawing groups of squares along the bottom of the entire building. Draw a small beacon on the top of the dome.

8

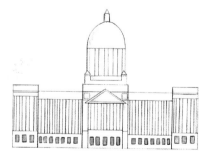

Finish the capitol by adding shading and erasing any extra lines. Color in the windows, as well.

29

State Facts

Statehood	June 1, 1792, 15th state
Area	40,411 square miles (104,664 sq km)
Population	3,960,800
Capital	Frankfort, population 26,700
Most Populated City	Louisville, population 271,000
Industries	Manufacturing, government, finance, insurance, real estate, retail trade
Agriculture	Tobacco, horses, cattle, corn, dairy
Tree	Tulip tree
Game animal	Gray squirrel
Rock	Kentucky agate
Language	English
Nicknames	The Bluegrass State, the Tobacco State
Motto	United We Stand, Divided We Fall
Bird	Cardinal
Flower	Goldenrod
Fossil	Brachiopod
Gemstone	Freshwater pearl
Horse	Thoroughbred
Butterfly	Viceroy butterfly
Fish	Kentucky bass

Glossary

American Revolution (uh-MER-uh-ken reh-vuh-LOO-shun) Battles that soldiers from the colonies fought against England for freedom.

architecture (AR-kih-tek-chur) The science, art, or profession of designing buildings.

assassinated (uh-SA-sin-ayt-ed) To have murdered an important or famous person.

bronze (BRONZ) A golden brown blend of copper and tin metals.

Civil War (SIH-vul WOR) The war fought between the northern and southern states of America from 1861 to 1865.

Confederate States (kun-FEH-duh-ret STAYTS) States that fought for the South during the Civil War.

crest (KREST) A head decoration on a bird.

diameter (dy-A-meh-tur) The measurement across the center of a round object.

frontier (frun-TEER) The edge of a settled country, where the wilderness begins.

malice (MA-lihs) The desire to cause harm or pain to someone.

memorial (meh-MOR-ee-uhl) A reminder of a person or an event.

pioneer (py-uh-NEER) One of the first people to settle in a new area.

plateau (pla-TOH) A flat area of land.

rival (RY-vuhl) To be the equal of.

rotunda (roh-TUN-dah) A round dome.

species (SPEE-sheez) A single kind of plant or animal. For example, all people are one species.

statesman (STAYTS-mun) A person who has shown skill or wisdom in politics or government.

thoroughbred (THER-oh-bred) An English breed of horse that is used for racing.

trills (TRILZ) Birdsong.

unified (YOO-nih-fyd) Joined together in a shared interest.

Index

Web Sites

To learn more about Kentucky, check out this Web site:
www.state.ky.us